Growing Green

A young person's guide to taking care of the planet

Christina Goodings

Masumi Furukawa

LION
CHILDREN'S

Contents

Growing greens
On the move
Faraway places
Clean green sea
Fair shares for all
A better world

Tread lightly

Next time you walk through long grass, turn around to look at the trail you have left. Can you see where your footprints have flattened the stems and squashed the leaves? Could you have chosen a better path – one that treated the plants more gently?

This book is not only about taking care of the grass. It is to show you the many ways we humans leave our mark: on the earth, in the air and upon the water.

This book will help you learn to tread lightly on the planet. Then all the earth will grow green.

all kinds of insects make their home in the grass

all kinds of flowers bloom beside the path

each tall tree
begins as a tiny
seedling

Less is more

The more you use, the more you take of what the world can give you. You are greedy for its resources.
The less you use, the less you take. You become a gentle user of the world's resources.

more, more and more things

just enough for me...   ... and something to share
with you

Before you buy something new, think: could you make do without it?
When you no longer want something, think: could someone else use it?

The gentle home

Even a very ordinary home is a paradise of luxuries.
It's so easy to use them all extravagantly.

bright light at the flick of a switch

clean and simple heat for easy cooking

cool clean water on tap

big trash can for everything

just throw it all away!

If you go camping, you notice how many resources you use for a very simple life.

how far is the supply of clean water

how little time a lantern shines

how the trash piles up

how heavy is the firewood

how the smoke smells

how quickly all the firewood burns

how will it get to the dump?

When you use light and heat and water at home, think: can you be more careful with resources? You would if you were camping.

A load of trash

What happens to the things you no longer want?

Some things can be reused:

Some things can be recycled:

jars for jam

jars for pencils

jars for paper clips
and brushes

What else could you reuse?

pack them
down small

sort papers
for collection

wash bottles

Fruit and vegetable waste can be composted.
Add it to a compost bin along with garden trimmings.

garden clippings

compost heap

kitchen
peelings

rich brown soil

contented worms

There isn't room for endless garbage.
Think of the ways you can put less on the trash heap.

Habitats

The world is not only a place for people. It is a place for all kinds of plants and all kinds of creatures.
It is important for them to have room to live and grow: their own habitats.

let the plants grow

even tiny
creatures are
part of the
way of life

Once all the world was a wild place. Think: how could you leave it a little wild for all the wild things there are?

let the flowers
scatter their seeds

let the birds
nest in the
trees

let the creatures live
their own lives

make a space for trees to grow tall

Thought for food

Our planet earth produces plenty of harvests.
Enjoy them wisely.

Choose a variety of natural foods:

fruit

bread

vegetables

rice

cheese

fish

eggs

Do you choose food that is processed and packaged?
Think: what foods could you choose that are simply themselves?

Does the food you buy come from far away?
Have people used fuel to bring it to you?

fruit in the orchards

cows in the meadow

where can you buy straight from the farm?

chickens pecking everywhere

Think: could you choose food that is produced closer to home?

Growing greens

When food is easy to buy, it is easy to waste. If you learn how to grow food and gather your own garden harvest, you will find out how much effort it takes.

big pots filled with soil will produce good crops

Think: what could you grow for yourself in a pot of earth or perhaps a whole garden?

A garden plot

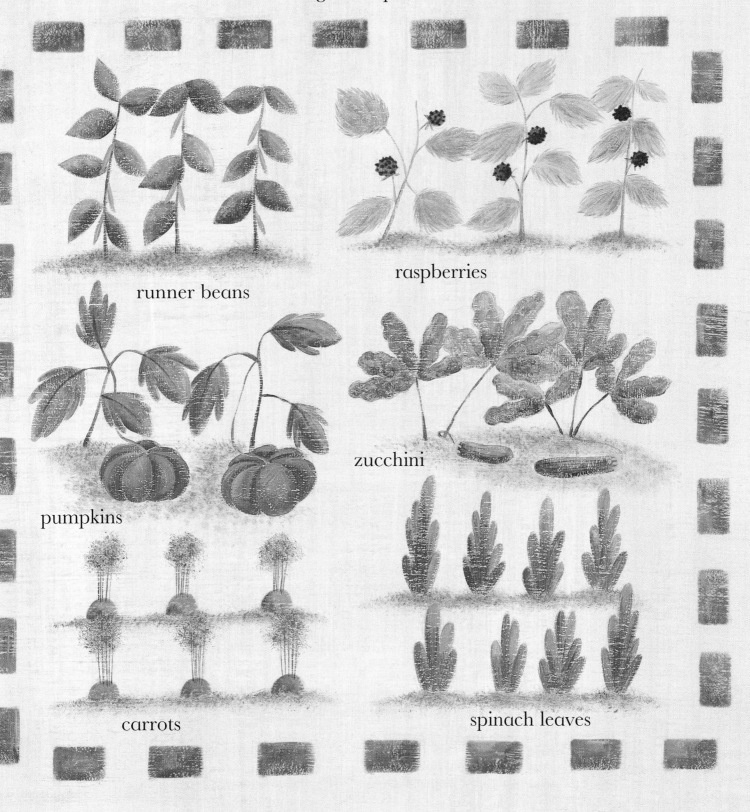

runner beans

raspberries

pumpkins

zucchini

carrots

spinach leaves

On the move

So many ways of getting around burn oil. But oil is getting scarcer. The fumes damage the atmosphere that surrounds our planet.

One of the damaging gases in the fumes is carbon dioxide.

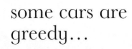

some cars are greedy…

… and some use clean electricity

does everyone need to go by car when there's a bus to share?

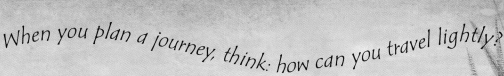

When you plan a journey, think: how can you travel lightly?

it takes a lot of fuel to fly you in the sky

use your own energy to travel: why not walk?

power your own wheels with your own food energy

Faraway places

All around the world, the plants and the creatures need space to thrive. But there are billions of people in the world today, and they are using more and more of the world's resources. Everyone needs to take care not to damage valuable habitats – even if they are far away.

Think, for example, of the rainforests, which grow near the equator and are home to many species. These include plants that can be used for medicines and rare and wonderful creatures.

Yet in many places, people are clearing the forest trees. The wood is used as timber; the cleared land is used for crops. Some types of habitat can seem a waste of space… marshes, perhaps, or moorland. But think of the many creatures and plants that need them… and we need a world with many different lifeforms: biodiversity.

rainforest

orangutan

It is easy to enjoy the things that money can buy.
But think: what are they costing the earth?

Clean green sea

Life depends on water. It is always on the move… from sea to cloud to rain to river to sea. It gives people and creatures what they need to drink. It allows the plants to grow roots and shoots, leaves and flowers, fruits and seeds. Enjoy water… but treat it with respect.

sunshine turns
water into vapor

clouds

rain and snow

water vapor

woods and fields let
rainwater trickle down

rivers

sea

clean water

The waste materials in trash heaps may dissolve in rainwater... and trickle
to the rivers. Think: don't let your trash pollute the world's water.

Fair shares for all

Where does it all come from? The food you eat, the clothes you wear… anything and everything.

All over the world, people are working to provide things you use.

It is only right that they should get a fair wage for their work.

It is only right that they should have opportunities for themselves and their children.

children going to school to learn

cocoa beans

Some people don't get paid a lot for picking cocoa. It is important to pay a fair price for your chocolate.

Enjoy what you buy, but think: are the workers being treated fairly?

A better world

When humankind lives gently and fairly, the world will be a better place. Dream of a time when all is well.

everyone has the food they need

everyone has clothes and shelter

the world has all grown green

the world's air is clean

young and old have a
chance to learn and to make
the most of who they are

the world's
water is clean

There will be a chance for peace.